EVENTS IN U.S. HISTORY

IMMIGRATION THROUGH

ELLIS ISLAND

by Christopher Forest

pogo

Ideas for Parents and Teachers

Pogo Books let children practice reading informational text while introducing them to nonfiction features such as headings, labels, sidebars, maps, and diagrams, as well as a table of contents, glossary, and index.

Carefully leveled text with a strong photo match offers early fluent readers the support they need to succeed.

Before Reading

- "Walk" through the book and point out the various nonfiction features. Ask the student what purpose each feature serves.
- Look at the glossary together. Read and discuss the words.

Read the Book

- Have the child read the book independently.
- Invite him or her to list questions that arise from reading.

After Reading

- Discuss the child's questions. Talk about how he or she might find answers to those questions.
- Prompt the child to think more. Ask: How has immigration changed the United States?

Pogo Books are published by Jump!
5357 Penn Avenue South
Minneapolis, MN 55419
www.jumplibrary.com

Library of Congress Cataloging-in-Publication Data

Names: Forest, Christopher, author.
Title: Immigration through Ellis Island by Christopher Forest.
Description: Minneapolis: Pogo Books, [2021]
Series: Turning points in U.S. history | Includes index.
Audience: Ages 7-10 | Audience: Grades 2-3
Identifiers: LCCN 2019047575 (print)
LCCN 2019047576 (ebook)
ISBN 9781645274315 (hardcover)
ISBN 9781645274322 (paperback)
ISBN 9781645274339 (ebook)
Subjects: LCSH: Ellis Island Immigration Station (N.Y. and N.J.)–History–Juvenile literature.
Ellis Island (N.J. and N.Y.)–History–Juvenile literature.
United States–Emigration and immigration–History–Juvenile literature.
Classification: LCC JV6484 .F67 2021 (print)
LCC JV6484 (ebook) | DDC 304.8/73–dc23
LC record available at https://lccn.loc.gov/2019047575
LC ebook record available at https://lccn.loc.gov/2019047576

Editor: Jenna Gleisner
Designer: Jenna Casura

Photo Credits: Everett Historical/Shutterstock, cover, 3, 16, 23; Universal History Archive/Getty, 1; Gado Images/Alamy, 4; Herb Quick/Alamy, 5; American Photo Archive/Alamy, 6-7; Everett Collection/Age Fotostock, 8; Sean Pavone/Alamy, 9; Bettmann/Getty, 10-11; Hi-Story/Alamy, 12-13; FPG/Getty, 14-15; Riccardo Sala/Alamy, 17; Mario Tama/Getty, 18-19; OlegAlbinsky/iStock, 20-21.

Printed in the United States of America at Corporate Graphics in North Mankato, Minnesota.

TABLE OF CONTENTS

CHAPTER 1

WELCOME TO ELLIS ISLAND

On January 1, 1892, Annie Moore arrived in the United States. She was only 17. She crossed the Atlantic Ocean from Queenstown, Ireland. The only way was by ship at the time. The **voyage** took 12 days.

immigration ship

Annie came to the United States for a better life. She was the first **immigrant** to arrive on Ellis Island. A **statue** of her stands in the museum there now.

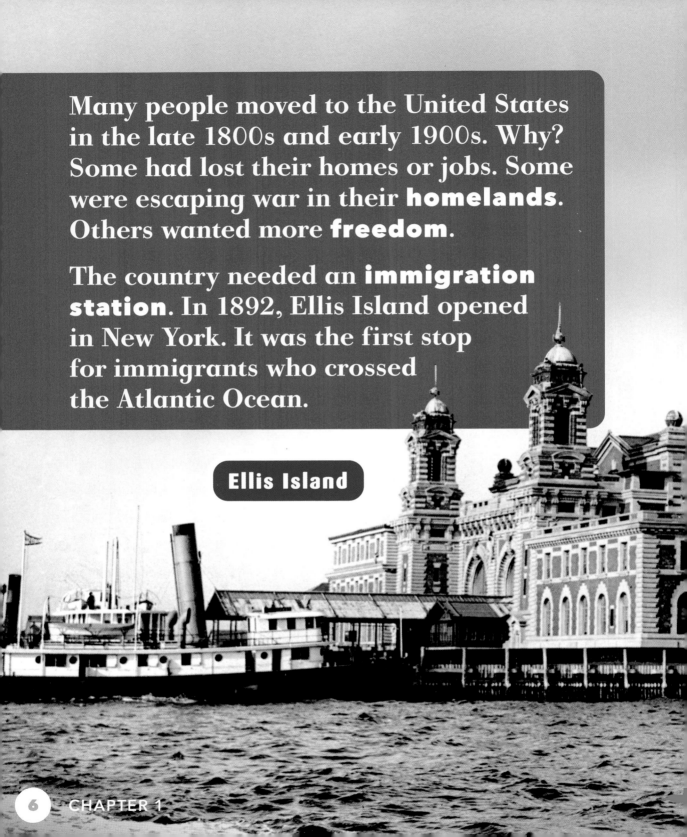

Many people moved to the United States in the late 1800s and early 1900s. Why? Some had lost their homes or jobs. Some were escaping war in their **homelands**. Others wanted more **freedom**.

The country needed an **immigration station**. In 1892, Ellis Island opened in New York. It was the first stop for immigrants who crossed the Atlantic Ocean.

Ellis Island

TAKE A LOOK!

Most immigrants came from Europe. Take a look at Annie's journey from Ireland. Can you imagine traveling this far by boat?

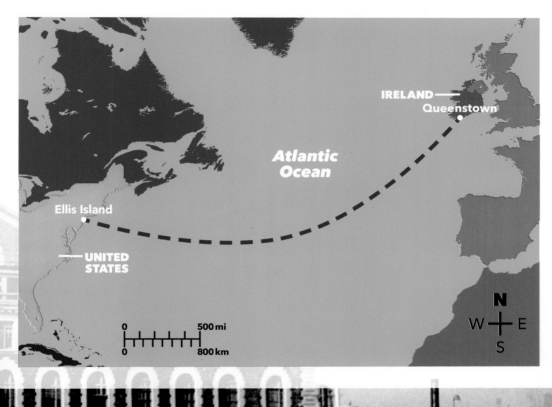

IRELAND

Queenstown

Atlantic Ocean

Ellis Island

UNITED STATES

N W E S

0   500 mi

0   800 km

CHAPTER 2

A LOOK INSIDE

Ellis Island was a busy place. Millions of people entered the country. They arrived with what they could carry.

They entered a large building. It was crowded and noisy. First stop was the Baggage Room. Belongings were left here. They were **inspected**. Bags from that time period are on display today.

Baggage Room

Next, they went to the Registry Room. Doctors examined all immigrants. Why? They wanted to make sure they were healthy. This stopped new diseases from spreading in the country.

WHAT DO YOU THINK?

Have you ever moved to a new place? How did it feel? If you haven't moved, think of someone who has. How do you think he or she felt?

inspector

What country are you from? What is your job? These are questions inspectors asked. Why? They wanted to stop dangerous people from coming into the country. Immigrants had to answer. Those who passed both exams became U.S. **citizens**!

Not everyone was able to enter right away. Some had to stay in the hospital until they got healthy. Inspectors also kept those they thought would need government help. Many were women and children. Women could not enter without a male relative.

WHAT DO YOU THINK?

Between 1892 and 1924, nearly 12 million immigrants came through Ellis Island. What opportunities do you think they were seeking?

CHAPTER 3
STARTING FRESH

Immigrants **settled** throughout the country. Some made a living by selling food. Others opened stores.

In 1924, new laws passed. Fewer people were allowed entry. In 1954, the government closed Ellis Island. It reopened in 1990. It is now a museum.

Ellis Island
Immigration Museum
Statue of Liberty National Monument

National Park Service
United States Department of the Interior

Many immigrants still come to the United States each year. They leave their homelands. Most have similar reasons to immigrants who came through Ellis Island. They work hard to become citizens. They help the United States grow.

TAKE A LOOK!

How many immigrants have come to the United States since Ellis Island opened? Take a look! When has the number increased and decreased? What events in history may have caused those changes?

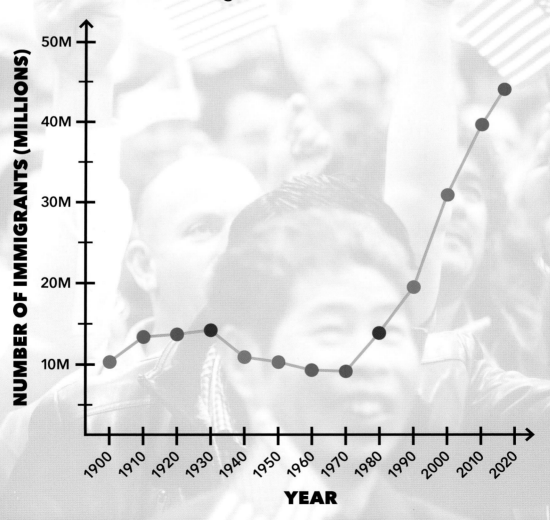

Ellis Island has been called the Isle of Hope. Millions of immigrants passed through. They came to start new lives. Today, people visit it. They learn about immigration as part of U.S. history.

They often visit the Statue of Liberty, too! This is another **symbol** of freedom. Would you like to visit Ellis Island?

Ellis Island

Statue of Liberty

QUICK FACTS & TOOLS

1924
A law is passed in the United States that drastically reduces the number of immigrants allowed into the country. Ellis Island is only used to hold immigrants who cannot immediately enter.

1892
Ellis Island opens on January 1. Annie Moore is the first person to enter the United States through the island.

1965
Ellis Island becomes part of the Statue of Liberty National Monument.

1954
Ellis Island closes in November.

1990
The Ellis Island Immigration Museum opens to the public.

1907
A record 11,747 immigrants arrive on April 17, 1907. More than 1.2 million immigrants arrive at Ellis Island in 1907.

GLOSSARY

citizens: People who have full rights in a certain country, such as the right to work and the right to vote.

freedom: The right or power to do and say what you like.

homelands: The countries or regions that you or your family come from.

immigrant: Someone who moves to settle permanently in another country.

immigration station: A place where officials check immigrants.

inspected: Checked or examined.

settled: Made a home or lived in a new place.

statue: A model of a person or an animal, especially one that is life-size or larger, made from metal, stone, wood, or any solid material.

symbol: An object or design that stands for, suggests, or represents something else.

voyage: A long journey by sea or in space.

INDEX

TO LEARN MORE

Finding more information is as easy as 1, 2, 3.

❶ Go to www.factsurfer.com

❷ Enter "immigrationthroughEllisIsland" into the search box.

❸ Choose your book to see a list of websites.

FACT SURFER